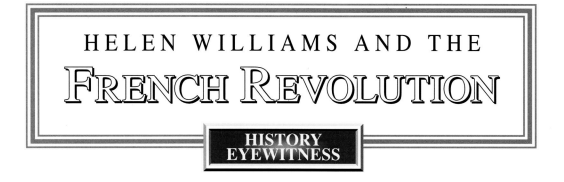

HELEN WILLIAMS AND THE
FRENCH REVOLUTION

**HISTORY
EYEWITNESS**

EDITED WITH AN INTRODUCTION
AND ADDITIONAL MATERIAL BY

JANE SHUTER

RSVP

**RAINTREE
STECK-VAUGHN**
PUBLISHERS
The Steck-Vaughn Company

Austin, Texas

Published by Raintree Steck-Vaughn Publishers, an imprint of Steck-Vaughn Company

Designed by Green Door Design Ltd.

Library of Congress Cataloging-in-Publication Data

Williams, Helen Maria, 1702–1827.
 Helen Williams and the French Revolution / edited with an introduction and additional material by Jane Shuter.
  p. cm. — (History eyewitness)
 Includes index.
 ISBN 0-8114-8287-1
 1. Williams, Helen Maria, 1762–1827 — Homes and haunts — France — Paris. 2. France — History — Revolution, 1789–1799 — Personal narratives. 3. France — History — Reign of terror, 1793–1794. 4. Robespierre, Maximilien, 1758–1794 — Death and burial. 5. Regicides. I. Shuter, Jane. II. Title. III. Series.
 DC146.W67A3 1996
 944.04'092—dc20   95-18350
                                              CIP
                                              AC

Printed in China
Bound in the United States
1 2 3 4 5 6 7 8 9 0 LB 99 98 97 96 95

Acknowledgments

The publishers would like to thank the following for permission to reproduce photographs:

Bridgeman Art Library: p.38
Bridgeman Art Library/Musée Carnavalet, Paris: pp.6, 10, 33
Bridgeman/Giraudon: pp.13, 35
Bridgeman/Musée des Beaux-Arts, Quimper: p.27
British Museum: p.16
E. T. Archive: p.23
Giraudon: pp.19, 24, 41, 45
Giraudon/Musée Carnavalet, Paris: cover and pp.15, 20, 30, 36
Photographie Bulloz: p.9
Phototèque des Musées de la Ville de Paris: pp.28, 43

The cover photograph shows the execution of Marie Antoinette.

Every effort has been made to contact copyright holders of material reproduced in this book. Any omissions will be rectified in subsequent printings if notice is given to the publisher.

Note to the Reader

In this book some of the words are printed in **bold** type. This indicates that the word is listed in the glossary on pages 46–47. The glossary gives a brief explanation of words that may be new to you.

CONTENTS

Introduction

The French Revolution and the Reign of Terror
The French Revolution was a reaction by the people of France to terrible living conditions that the rulers of the country were doing nothing to improve, which began on July 14, 1789. The Reign of Terror began on May 31, 1793. It is seen as ending on July 28, 1794, with the execution of Robespierre and his friends. Helen Williams can be confusing at times in her chronology. The timeline on page 5 will help to keep events in place. Some pages have a timeline box for the same reason.

Helen Maria Williams, 1762–1827
Helen Williams was born in London. When her father died, her family moved to Berwick-upon-Tweed. She returned to London in 1781 and stayed there, writing books and poetry. In 1788 she went to France to visit her sister, Cecilia, who was married to a Protestant minister. Helen Williams was in favor of the ideas of the French Revolution. She wrote enthusiastically about liberty and equality. She was a friend of many Girondists (see box on page 6). One of her closest friends was Madame Roland, who was executed during the Reign of Terror. Helen Williams and her family were arrested as foreigners and narrowly escaped execution. She lived for the rest of her life in Paris, except for the last few years of her life, which she spent with her nephew in Amsterdam. She asked to be buried in Paris.

Helen Williams lived in Paris during the Reign of Terror. This book is based on her *Letters Containing a Sketch of the Politics of France from May 31, 1793 to July 28, 1794*. She gives a firsthand view of life there — but it is a biased firsthand view. She was a middle-class foreign woman, and she saw the events of the Revolution and the Reign of Terror from her own viewpoint. So she said very little about the almost constant fighting between France and the rest of Europe at this time, except for vague references to brave soldiers. Many of her friends were executed by the Revolutionary government. She was herself arrested and feared that she, too, would be executed. So her experiences relate some of the horrors of the Reign of Terror. These horrors should neither be forgotten nor treated lightly.

Helen Williams wrote what she believed to be the truth. However, sometimes the things that she said were distorted by her own opinions, or by the fact that she was given wrong information. Where research has shown that her account is inaccurate, it has been pointed out in the information boxes.

The French Revolution and the Reign of Terror

The following dates provide a framework for Helen Williams's story. One of the things that they show is that the guillotine and much of the government structure that was part of the Reign of Terror (the Revolutionary Tribunal, the Committee of Public Safety) were already set up before the events of May 31 to June 2, 1793.

July 14, 1789	The Bastille was stormed; the French Revolution began.
July/August 1789	The first wave of émigrés left France.
September 22, 1791	France became a republic.
August 17, 1792	Robespierre was on the Committee that ran the Paris Commune.
September 1792	September massacres; prisoners killed because of fears of invasion. The second wave of émigrés left France.
September 22, 1792	The New Calendar was announced.
January 21, 1793	Louis XVI was executed.
March 10, 1793	The Revolutionary Tribunal was set up to deal quickly with "counterrevolutionary" crimes. Revolutionary committees were also set up for local administration. They were to be checked upon by a revolutionary army.
April 6, 1793	The Committee of Public Safety was set up.
May 31–June 2, 1793	THE REIGN OF TERROR BEGAN The period when France was governed by people who paid less and less attention to justice. More and more, they used the guillotine to punish any sort of crime, even only suspected ones, causing terror among the people.
July 27, 1793	Robespierre was elected to sit on the Committee of Public Safety.
October 16, 1793	Marie Antoinette was executed.
October 1793	Helen Williams was arrested.
October 31, 1793	The 22 deputies from the old Convention were executed.
Late November 1793	Helen Williams was released.
March 1794	The arrest of deputies who had worked closely with Robespierre to replace the old Convention — Hébert, Danton, Desmoulins, La Croix, and others
April 5, 1794	These deputies were executed.
April 16, 1794	Foreigners and nobles were forced to leave cities and ports.
May 7, 1794	A new religion, worship of the Supreme Being, set up by Robespierre
May 24, 1794	Failed assassination attempt on Robespierre
June 4, 1794	Robespierre was made President of the Convention.
June 8, 1794	Festival of the Supreme Being
June 10, 1794	Decree made execution without trial legal.
July 3, 1794	Robespierre, angry at opposition in the Convention, refused to attend the meetings for several days. During this time, the Convention worked quickly to act against him.
July 27, 1794	Robespierre and his friends were arrested, by order of the Convention. They were taken to the Luxembourg prison, where the jailer let them go. They made their way to the Town Hall. The Paris Commune was not sure whether to help them or not. While they wondered, the Convention issued a decree that made Robespierre and his friends outlaws. Now it would be very dangerous to help them.
July 28, 1794	Robespierre and his friends were arrested again and executed without trial. THE REIGN OF TERROR ENDED
July 29, 1794	More of Robespierre's supporters were executed.
August 1794	A new Convention was elected, one with more moderate men.

CHAPTER 1

After the Revolution

I feel I should tell you of the events that led to the onset of the Reign of Terror. There was much talk of liberty still. The old **National Assembly** was now the **National Convention**. There were some who feared that some unscrupulous people might try to seize power in these confused times. The representatives of the people in the Convention could not agree. The republicans wanted to moderate the reforms. Others thought that the reforms had not gone far enough. But the reformers thought that any discontent was just from making changes too quickly. They would be accepted. They did not see the danger of other, more radical groups. Chief among these was the **Paris Commune**, whose members thought they had equal claims with the **Jacobins** to have set the Revolution in motion. The Commune set itself up as a rival power, even before the first Convention had met. It was in the Commune that Robespierre and his fellow conspirators first rose to power. At first, the Convention left the Commune alone, but then the Convention saw that it had to act.

POLITICAL PARTIES

The political groups in France at this time can be difficult to distinguish. Their aims changed, and people often moved from group to group. The main ones were:

Girondists
The **Girondists** wanted a republic. But they were moderate men, who wanted moderate reforms. They had the most members in the Convention in 1793.

Montagnards
The **Montagnards** were a smaller group and were more extreme in their views. It was this group that controlled the Convention during the Reign of Terror.

The French Revolution began with the storming of the Bastille, July 14, 1789. This picture shows the arrest of the governor of the Bastille, after it was captured. He was executed some hours after his arrest.

There were revolts in the country, too, but the Revolution and the Reign of Terror centered on Paris. This was where the National Assembly, later renamed the National Convention, met. It was where laws were made, and the country was run from.

It was clear that the Convention had to deal with the crimes committed by the Commune. The Convention could not let these crimes and the further atrocities that the members of the Commune had planned go unpunished. There were trials, but they were badly held. There were executions, but of the wrong people. The Convention did not distinguish between the chiefs of the conspiracy and those who had been sucked in. And while others suffered, Robespierre made his next move. He had gained power in the Commune but saw that people wanted the Convention to govern. So he proceeded to get himself a place there, too, with the same aim as before, absolute power.

Robespierre and his faction took over the Jacobin name and used it as a disguise for their own plans, filling the Jacobin clubs, especially those in Paris, with ambitious and unscrupulous men. They took over the running of Paris through the Paris Commune and set to work, secretly, to get support in the **local administration**. There were few of them in the Convention, yet they still had a lot of influence and power. The Convention granted some of their requests, hoping to satisfy them, but with each concession, they grew more greedy. There were those in the Convention who warned others of their rise, but they were ignored. Most members of the Convention could not believe that anyone would use the Jacobin name in such a way. Their first moves against the Convention should have been treated as **rebellion**, but there was too high of a regard for **individual liberties** at this time. So they did not act until too late. Had they acted sooner, they would have saved themselves and the people of France a great deal of sorrow.

TIMESCALE
Helen Williams begins her life story during the Reign of Terror in March 1793. At this point, France was being governed by a National Convention and had officially become a republic on September 22, 1791.

The new French flag was the tricolor, made up of red, white, and blue stripes. Ribbons and badges were also made out of these three colors, which all patriotic people were expected to wear.

The King, Louis XVI, had been made into an ordinary citizen, Citizen Capet. But he was too much of a focus for royalist hopes to be left alive. He was executed on January 21, 1792.

Dumouriez was one of the commanders of the French Army. France was at war almost entirely throughout the Revolution and the Reign of Terror. The other European countries saw the French Revolution as dangerous. They feared the spirit of independence might spread to them. So they attacked France in several places at once, hoping to beat the French and bring back the monarchy.

Dumouriez was angry at the way the government treated the army. He felt that the government was too concerned with politics and not concerned enough with the war. Commanders were appointed for their "revolutionary fervor," not for their skills at commanding. Those who were defeated in battle were often arrested, no matter how high the odds had been against their winning.

The Convention heard that Dumouriez was negotiating with the Austrian commander. He fled to Austria and was declared a traitor.

The **treason** of Dumouriez gave the **faction** some power over the republicans, especially because he had friends in the Convention. The Jacobins said this tarred all with the same brush. Robespierre's faction wanted to control not just the Jacobins or the Paris Commune, but the Convention itself. The faction could not succeed while the elected representatives were there, so they had to blacken the names of the representatives and seize power. The faction arranged to have **petitions** sent to the Convention by people seemingly unconnected with them, begging for the removal of certain Convention members. But the Convention was suspicious. They held an **inquiry** about the petitions. The petitions were traced back to Hébert, one of the Paris Commune. The conspirators, seeing that they were about to be found out, threw off the mask and brought the whole Commune to demand the end of the inquiry and the arrest not only of the 22 **deputies** listed on the petition, but also of all the people who had taken part in the inquiry about the petitions. The Convention refused. President Isnard demanded that the Commune withdraw their demands. But the chiefs of the conspiracy had gone too far to back out now. They rang bells, fired cannons, and beat drums, calling the people of Paris to rise. The National Guard armed themselves, and, led by Hanriot, not yet knowing who their enemy was, were taken to the Convention to besiege it.

Yet the assault on the Convention, begun on May 31, did not get the conspirators what they wanted right away. Robespierre and his revolutionary women stood guard by the Hall where the Convention met; no one was allowed to leave. The people were prepared for a fresh attack. On June 1, the building was attacked by 60,000 men. It is unlikely that everyone who helped the conspirators realized how far they intended to go; people were swept along by the tide of events. At last Hanriot announced that if the 22 deputies were not given up, he would fire the cannon on the building. The President proposed leaving the Hall. All rose, and the guard at the door fell back, outnumbered. They got as far as the garden but could go no further. Robespierre persuaded them to return to the Hall to make a decision. They went back. Now many of them thought it would be best to give up the 22, and they were asked to give themselves up for the sake of their country. Some agreed, but others refused, saying that if they left, the conspirators would gain more power. If only they had stood firm. If only they had demanded the execution of the conspirators and Hanriot. But they did not. They agreed, to prevent bloodshed! What irony, when you think of what was to come. And the people had no way of knowing what was going on. We had seen the Hall surrounded. We had seen the Convention walk into the grounds, speak with Robespierre, and return— yet we had no grasp on what this all meant.

Immediately after June 2, the **Committee of Public Safety** published an address to "calm and inform the people." Most of the Convention protested, and 73 of them signed a petition against it. This was never published, so we never knew of their objections. By now, the rest of France had heard of what had happened to the Convention and sent messengers to ask how it could be that their elected representatives could be kept as prisoners and treated as traitors. Yet the people of Paris were reacting strangely. It seemed as though they felt that only a king could be a tyrant, so it did not much matter, otherwise, who ruled. Had they thought more and acted, so many of their fellow citizens would have been spared the scaffold. The conspirators had, as I have said, managed to get people into many of the local citizens groups. They swayed the actions of many groups. The people followed without thinking. They, too, demanded the expulsion of the 22 deputies, tricked into believing that this was a just demand. The **départements** were more watchful, but they had no real power to affect events, and the messages they sent arrived both garbled and too late. There was some talk that the départements might march on Paris, but it came to nothing. The conspirators had the big advantage, because they controlled the machinery of the government as well as the National Guard. The départements had less money, less authority, fewer arms, and no centralized organization. And so the whole republic, except for uprisings in the Vendée, and in a few cities such as Lyons and Toulon, gave in to the conspirators, fearing **civil war**. The conspirators quickly produced a **constitution**, which made them popular. The Revolutionary government was proclaimed, and all acts were now justifiable in its name.

An inkwell showing a priest crushed by the red cap of liberty. Priests were seen as greedy, because a tenth of everything a person earned or grew had to go to the local priest. The symbols of liberty were the red cap, a bundle of sticks (to remind people of the Roman republic, which used this symbol) and the tricolor. Clothes, even wallpaper and furniture, were made using them.

CHAPTER 2

The Vendée

There was resistance to both the Revolution and the conspirators. Some towns held out, but the most dangerous resistance was in the **Vendée**. I will deal with the rising in the Vendée all at once, not at the various times at which it arose.

The Vendée was an uprising that aimed to replace the **monarchy**. It was led by priests, who had not done well after the Revolution. It had an army of some 40,000 men, led by some of the best army leaders from the old days. While the Jacobins were taking over in Paris, the Vendéan army was seizing alarmingly large parts of the countryside. They felt strong enough to send a list of demands around the country, asking for the return of the monarchy and the Catholic religion. At this point, the Convention was roused to action and sent 3,000 men against them. Yet they did not try hard to beat the **royalists**. They had their own devious reasons for this.

Some of the 22 deputies had escaped to the provinces, and the conspirators wanted to accuse them of joining the royalists. Once the conspirators became the Revolutionary government, they could really crush the Vendéans. Their army was so badly organized that it is hard to see how the Revolutionary government could have watched their antics for as long as they did. At last they issued a **decree** that the war would be won by October 20. Strange as it seemed, it won the war, partly because the decree also ordered the burning of crops, homes, and whole towns until the war was won. There followed wholesale destruction, massacre, and plunder.

This picture shows the National Guard swearing the Patriotic Oath to support the principles of the Revolution. Many pictures like this were painted at the time, giving the impression that the Revolution had the support of all the people of France. In the early days of the Revolution, priests were still allowed to hold services, even though the Church was not allowed to own property. The image here suggests that the priests and the people all worked together to support the principles of the Revolution. As we can see from the uprising in the Vendée, not everyone supported the Revolution, even in its early days.

CHAPTER 3

Marat Stabbed!

Something else happened that was to seal the fate of the deputies, already accused of joining the uprising in the Vendée. This was the **assassination** of Marat. Marat had been involved with the conspirators from the beginning. They used him as the mouthpiece for their lies against honest and decent men. He was the joker of the Convention — loudmouthed, extravagant, deformed, and often labeled a fool. The general effect that he had on people was to make them feel the kind of dislike you feel for a loathsome reptile. His political beliefs varied, according to what people wanted him to say. What made him really useful to the conspirators was his willingness to pass on any slander they pleased and to support any horror that they suggested. Indeed, so keen was he to **denounce** traitors that he was often tricked into standing up and denouncing imaginary people who had been made up by those with nothing better to do than to tease him.

Marat had become very ill. He had some progressing disease and was forced to stay in his room. The disease would probably soon have killed him. But he was assassinated in his bathtub by a young woman, Charlotte Corday, who had come from Caen in Normandy just to do this. She was the daughter of a historian and a believer in the **republic** and liberty. She felt that if she could assassinate Marat, she would save France.

She came to Paris and made an excuse to see Marat. Taking out a knife that she had bought for the occasion, she plunged it into his chest. She was immediately arrested and taken to the Abbaye prison, then transferred to the Conciergerie, from where she was brought before the **Revolutionary Tribunal**. She confessed to the deed, saying that she owed it to her country and to humankind to rid the world of a monster who was pushing the country toward bloodshed and civil war. She said she hoped to inspire people by her actions, for she loved her country more than her life. She was modest and dignified all through the trial and was so sweet to look at that you could not imagine her committing the crime. She replied forcefully to the questions of the Revolutionary Tribunal, surprising people with her wit and elegant expressions.

At the end of her trial, Charlotte Corday gave the judges three letters, two for the republican Barbaroux, who she had visited before the assassination, and one for her father. Barbaroux claimed she had not said what she was going to do. Had she done so, he said, he would have pointed her at a more worthwhile target. She was taken out while the jury deliberated. She was quite calm when she came back in and listened to her sentence attentively. Then she spoke to her lawyer for a moment, gave a friend of mine, who was sitting near, money to pay her few bills, and left the court.

THE REVOLUTIONARY TRIBUNAL

The Revolutionary Tribunal was set up on March 10, 1793. It was a special court, set up to deal with what were called "counterrevolutionary" crimes. These were crimes against the ideas of the republic, such as liberty and equality. They were also crimes that might threaten to end the republic, such as trying to bring back monarchy. The first Revolutionary Tribunal consisted of a jury, five judges, and a public prosecutor.

The Convention also set up revolutionary committees of twelve men in small local areas all through France, in Paris and in the départements, who were to make sure that the area was working in the way that the Revolutionary government wanted. They also dealt with all the people who were new arrivals in the area.

It is hard to describe the heroism that Charlotte Corday showed on the way to her execution. The women known as "the Furies of the Guillotine" had gathered together in order to insult her on the way to the guillotine, as they did with every execution. Even they were awed into silence by the dignified way that she behaved. Some spectators took their hats off to her; some others even applauded. She climbed the scaffold with undaunted firmness, resolved to die with dignity. Her jailer had told her how she was to die, but not all of the details of the process. But she did all that she was told and bowed her neck to the fatal stroke.

The leaders of the conspirators, who had earlier abandoned Marat to die when they thought he was of little more use to them, now proclaimed him a revolutionary martyr. They said his assassination was part of a far larger plot by the départements. This plot, they told the people, had been set up by the deputies, some of whom were now caught and in prison, to kill off the leaders of the Revolutionary government, one by one.

So, in this way, Marat became a hero, and the people began to think of those poor imprisoned men as traitors. This was the first cunning step in making sure that the people accepted their execution when the moment for their deaths finally came.

A painting by David, showing Marat dead in his bathtub. David was a supporter of the Revolutionary government. He shows Marat as being far from the deformed monster that Helen Williams describes in the text. The truth is probably somewhere between the two. Helen Williams would, after all, be likely to think the worst of Marat. Marat is known to have had a bad skin disease, which meant he had to spend a lot of his time in salt baths. He is unlikely to have been as smooth-skinned as David shows. This was all part of the campaign of the Revolutionary government to show Marat as a martyr and a hero.

Growing Suspicion

At the same time that the Revolutionary Tribunal was set up, in March 1793, revolutionary committees were set up all through France, consisting of twelve local people, who ran their area.

The revolutionary army, set up at the same time, must not be confused with the army of France. They were not soldiers, but men with the right "revolutionary spirit," who were sent to check that the revolutionary committees outside of Paris were running things in keeping with the Revolution.

The members of the revolutionary army were given specific areas to run. How severe they were varied widely from area to area, depending on who was in charge.

From the moment the Revolutionary government came to power, the atmosphere in Paris thickened with growing suspicion. Every day there were new plots discovered. These plots were laid at the door of, in order: nobles, priests, bankers, and foreigners. They were expected and hardly paid attention to. The stories became so feeble that they did little credit to the powers of invention of those who thought them up. Sometimes these stories were supported by letters that were supposed to be from foreign agents, but they were so badly forged that they convinced no one.

As soon as the départements accepted the Revolutionary government, the government began to act against all of those who had acted against it. And it was now that the phrase suspected came into use. Now you could be arrested on suspicion of being involved in a plot — arrested, that is, with no proof at all of your involvement in the matter. A decree was issued against all "suspected" of acting against the Revolutionary government. The members of the Revolutionary Tribunal protested at the broad sweep of this. They were accused of moderation and were replaced with men who were willing to do as they were told.

Now, too, was the time to clear away other groups that may have been useful in the Revolutionary government's rise to power but which were needed no more. Among these was a certain group of women who called themselves, "revolutionary women." These women came mainly from the lower classes, and they had served the conspirators well in their time. They held their own meetings and then sent members to influence the local committees in favor of the conspirators. In the days from May 30 to June 2, they had mounted guard on the Convention. But now they became overconfident. They came to the Revolutionary government with a list of demands — the exclusion of former nobles from any job in the government or rank in the army. All of those who worked for the government should be forced to confirm their allegiance to liberty, every suspected person should be arrested, women should be allowed to wear red caps (the symbol of liberty). This was too much, even for the new Convention of the Revolutionary government. The women's groups were disbanded by decree.

The Revolutionary government also decided that **revolutionary committees** should be set up in each section of Paris and all through the départements, to keep order and make sure the decrees of the government were carried out. There were fears that the revolutionary committees in the countryside might not be active enough. A **revolutionary army** was set up to go into the countryside to check up on the committees.

madameveto avait promi
de faire egorger tout paris
mais son cou amanque
grace a nos canonier
danson la carmagnole
Vive le son Vive le son
danson la carmagnole
Vive le son du canon

*The symbols of
liberty — the red cap,
the bundle of sticks,
and the tricolor
were everywhere in
Revolutionary France.*

*This plate, decorated with
symbols of liberty, has one of
the verses of a popular song during
the Revolution,* The Carmagnole,
*painted on it. The song celebrated
the storming of the Bastille and the
execution of Marie Antoinette, wife
of Louis XVI, who was nicknamed
"Madame Veto," because it was
said she always vetoed (refused to
accept) laws that would improve
the lives of the poor.*

*A translation of the words on the
plate is as follows:
"Madame Veto has promised
To have all Paris slaughtered
But now thanks to our cannoneers
It's her neck that's missing,
Dance the Carmagnole."*

Meanwhile,
the usurpers
(the Revolutionary
government) prepared to
bring the deputies that they had in prison to trial. They also arrested
the 73 deputies who had signed the petition against them. They then
said it would be impossible to sort the country out within the bounds
of the constitution. The new Convention voted to set aside the
constitution and allow the Revolutionary government to go their own
way. To reconcile the nation with this, the conspirators decided to act
against those the people hated — the aristocracy and foreigners. The
aristocracy was now not just the nobles. There was an aristocracy of
talents (the professions) and an aristocracy of commerce (businessmen).
They introduced "the maximum," a standard pricing policy for all
things [May 1973]. This was bound to be bad for trade and likely to
create more evils than it solved, but it was popular with the lower
classes, and that was what mattered to the Revolutionary government
at that time.

CHAPTER 5

Arrested!

This is how the English cartoonist, Gilray, saw the French Revolution. Despite Helen Williams's shock at the way the French reacted to foreigners, it is hardly a surprising response, considering the fact that most of the rest of Europe had declared war on France. Cartoons such as this were common.

One evening I was drinking tea with some French friends. Another friend rushed in to say that it had been decreed that all English people living in France would lose their property, and they would be arrested. This was contrary to a decree some days previously that had said we would not be harmed. We passed the night without sleep and were anxious all the following day, expecting that the local revolutionary committee would send soldiers to arrest us. As the day wore on, our terror increased, as we heard of more and more of our friends being arrested. When night fell, we began to think that, as a family of women, we were to be spared. But this was a time when neither age nor sex won you compassion. We were awakened in the middle of the night by a loud knocking at the door of our apartment; then the bell was rung loudly. There were two soldiers and two representatives of the revolutionary committee. While the soldiers stood guard outside, the others came in. One sternly said he would read us the decree. We replied that we knew of it and would obey the law. Seeing us pale, shaking, and obedient, they were kinder to us, saying our arrest was a general political measure and that the innocent had nothing to fear.

They took details of names, ages, and time of residence in France. Then they let us fetch only as much clean linen as fitted in a handkerchief. The doors to our rooms were sealed, and we were taken to the Committee Room. The place was crowded with soldiers and representatives, sleeping, reading, and eating. On our arrival some made revolutionary jokes in our hearing. Every half hour or so, more English prisoners were brought in. We were the only women among them. We stayed the night there. In the morning, our countrymen were led away, but we were kept behind. This was due to the kindness of those who had arrested us, who asked that we should not be sent to Madelonettes prison with the men, where there was hardly a bed between two, but that we should go to Luxembourg prison, in the old palace. This is where we were sent the next night. The keeper of the prison, Beniot, was a kind man, who many a wretch has blessed for the "crime" of compassion. Yet he was ill-suited to the job, for while he helped his prisoners as much as he could, he could not help them as much as he wished. We were put in a room of our own, threw ourselves on the mattresses in the corner, and slept.

We found the prison to be full of people of different classes, nationalities, and opinions. We met many who had previously had power and been tyrants in their turn, like Amelot, once a **minister** of Louis XVI. Prison life had a routine. In the morning, we did the jobs that needed doing — sweeping, making beds, and lighting fires. The afternoon was our own time. As the prison filled up, we were no longer alone in our room. Each big room had its own rules, which varied from room to room, depending on the occupants. We were, whoever we had been, all equal here, and soon became, like it or not, friends. Most people shared what they had with the people in their room, sometimes with others, too. A broom that a countess had brought with her swept the whole prison, and my kettle was never allowed to cool. As the number of prisoners rose, so the rules changed. In less than a week, the number went from 100 to 1,000. In the beginning, we were allowed visitors, letters, newspapers, and outside exercise. But, one by one, these privileges were taken from us.

The most frightful part of our imprisonment were the visits by Hanriot, leader of the military force in Paris, he who was ready to fire the cannon at the Convention. We first met him on the second day of our imprisonment. He came three or four times a week. He would burst into a room, waving his sword, accompanied by several guards. He swore and raved and acted as if his dearest wish was to drink our blood. He would yell about guillotines and executions, until at least one person fainted. Then he would leave.

PRISONS

The state of prisons at this time varied widely. The worst prisons were those that had been used as prisons before the Revolution, and which had dungeons, thick stone walls, and poor lighting. Probably the worst one of them all was Bicêtre (see picture, pages 24–25). The most feared, by many people, was the Conciergerie. This was because, from very early in the Revolution, when executions were not common, this was seen as the prison that no one got released from. As the Reign of Terror took hold, it was the stepping-stone to the gallows. Prisoners were collected from other prisons and moved to the Conciergerie for the last days, or even hours, before their execution.

Less frightening than the visits of Hanriot, but still unpleasant, were the visits of the administrator of police. His visits were full of smaller brutalities and cruelties and usually added a new restriction to our imprisonment. We were still, from time to time, allowed one evening paper for the whole prison. At first, we would snatch at it eagerly for news, but it soon became clear to us why we were still allowed it — we got no joy from it. Every line was stamped with conspiracy, vengeance, desolation, and death, and our reading was often such that it deprived us of sleep. Soon we chose not to read it.

One thing brought some of the prisoners cheer. This was the fact that the prison soon became home to those who had been tyrants more recently than those like Amelot, who had been tyrants under the king. These men had been tyrants of the Revolution but had been overtaken by the speed of the Revolution and had themselves become "suspect." One of these, a Monsieur Mallart, had just a few days before been responsible for the arrest of two of the boys in our room. They could not resist crowing over him when he arrived, whereas most arrivals were greeted with sympathy and concern.

There was something that brought us both risk and cheer. Our room led onto a small passage that had one other door in it, which was usually locked. The room it led to was inhabited by two men, called Sillery and Lasource, two of the 22 deputies who had been so misrepresented by the Revolutionary government. They were not allowed to mix with the other prisoners, but Sillery was sick, and two servants were allowed to come to the prison to care for him. The door to the passage was now unlocked to allow the servants to come and go, and this is how Lasource managed to make his way to our room. We had known both men well when they were free, and it was a pleasure to talk to him again. We had to speak in whispers, one of us always keeping watch at the door, in case someone came by. He had been in prison for three months, so there was much news from outside to give him. He managed to make his way to visit us each night and brought Sillery with him on his later visits. He was older and more resigned to his fate than Lasource. Lasource often spoke regretfully of his wife. They had been married for just one week before he was chosen as a member of the Legislative Assembly. He came to Paris, and she stayed behind to care for her old mother. Then he was chosen for the National Convention, and from that all else had followed, and he had never been able to see her again. It was hard to meet and to talk with them, knowing what their fate would be. And it was dangerous, too, but how could we refuse to take the risk for these our friends? Luckily they had their religion to keep their spirits up and had composed their own hymn, which they sang softly together before falling asleep each night.

THE FAUBOURGS OF PARIS

Faubourg was the name given to part of a French city that lay outside the city walls. However, cities tended to grow. Even by the fifteenth century, Paris had two city walls on its north side.

So faubourg came to mean a part of Paris that was not in the heart of the city, but which might — or might not — be inside the new city walls. Saint Antoine was inside them, part of the city, and governed by its laws.

At last, the morning of the trial arrived. Sillery and Lasource were collected to go with nineteen other members of the old Convention to be tried by the Revolutionary Tribunal. They were brought back at five in the evening, and that night they came to tell us what had happened. The judge and jury, they said, were obviously set on finding them guilty, not on giving the deputies a fair trial. They barely bothered to listen to the defense that the deputies presented. It was clear that they would be condemned.

A few days before their trial was to end, it was decreed that all of the Englishwomen imprisoned in the Luxembourg were to be moved to the prison in the **faubourg**, Saint Antoine. Sillery and Lasource regretted this, and so did we. They thanked us over and over for taking the risk of allowing them to visit. Sillery and Lasource each gave us a lock of their hair for us to remember them by. We never saw them again, though we heard later of their executions. It is appalling that men like them, who were such supporters of liberty should end their lives on the scaffold, under the sharp bite of the guillotine.

Helen Williams found that her life in prison became more uncomfortable. Even so, the conditions never got as bad as those in prisons like the Conciergerie, which was a prison that was known to be one that fed the guillotine more and more regularly as the Reign of Terror took hold.

This picture, painted at the time, is called Roll Call of the Condemned. *The man to the left with the red sash is reading out the names of those who are condemned to die. These people are then led out of the prison and loaded onto waiting carts, which take them to the guillotine. The soldier in the blue coat on the left is tearing a mother away from her daughters. People had to spend weeks, even months sometimes in these prison cells, with no privacy or sanitation, and very little light or food.*

CHAPTER 6

Marie Antoinette Executed!

The Revolutionary government, armed with the power that they had stolen, now tried to tighten their grip on the country even more. They fixed prices, forbade foreign trade, and acted against the aristocracy. They had been wanting to execute Marie Antoinette for a long time; now they arranged her trial. She was accused of an extraordinarily long list of crimes. At her trial, she replied to one of the accusations, which was of hurting her children, "I appeal to the conscience of every mother present. There cannot be one among you who does not shudder at the horror of such an accusation. Well, I am a mother, too."

Apart from this outburst, Marie Antoinette was calm all through the trial, refusing to answer the allegations, saying that no proof had been produced to back any of them up, so how could she disprove them? Robespierre certainly feared that the accusations may have gone too far, and might even win her public sympathy.

But nothing could save her, not all the sympathy in the world. She was condemned at about four o'clock in the morning and heard her sentence with composure. But her firmness of purpose left her as she was led from the court to the dungeons. She burst into tears and then, seeming ashamed of this natural reaction, turned to her guards and told them that while she might weep at this moment, in near privacy, they would not see her shed a single tear on her way to the scaffold.

She was taken to execution in the usual way, in a cart with her hair cut and with her hands tied behind her. She paid little attention to the priest who went with her, and still less to the surrounding mob. But the mob was mad with excitement, and her eyes did not conceal the emotion of her heart. Her cheeks seemed streaked with red at times; at others, she looked deathly pale. Her general look was of indignant sorrow.

It took until about noon for the procession to reach the place of execution. When Marie Antoinette set eyes on the palace and its gardens, where she had once lived and strolled, she seemed to become very agitated. She almost ran up the steps of the scaffold, and after what seemed but a few moments, her head was held up by the executioner for the people to see.

MARIE ANTOINETTE
Marie Antoinette was the wife of Louis XVI of France. She was an Austrian princess and had never been very popular with the French people. She spent money wildly, spending vast sums on clothes, jewels, and building beautiful gardens. Louis XVI was not strong-willed enough to stop her extravagance, and no one else could.

She was given nicknames that left her in no doubt about how unpopular she was: "Madame Deficit," "Madame Veto," and "L'Autricienne," referring, in turn, to her wild spending, her refusal to consider reform, and her nationality. This made her try to change her ways, to cut back on spending most of all. But by the time she did this her reputation was fixed. She could do nothing to change the way people saw her.

A drawing of the execution of Marie Antoinette, which was supposedly made at the time. Certainly the details of the guillotine and the method of execution are right. The victims' hair was cut short. Their hands were tied behind them, and when they reached the scaffold, their feet were tied to a plank. This was to keep them from kicking.

21

CHAPTER 7

Execution of the Deputies

The trial of Marie Antoinette was soon followed by the trial and execution of the deputies who had been so long **maligned**, hunted, and imprisoned. It was amazing that the trials had been left for so long, for Robespierre and the others wanted to be rid of these "enemies of the people." But not surprisingly under the circumstances, they were having difficulty getting any proof of treason against these men. They could find no evidence — which considering how honest these men were, and how hard they had labored for liberty before the Revolution and until their arrest, it seemed improbable that the conspirators would ever find any proof.

The Revolutionary government was not even sure just what to **charge** them with, or who they would be said to have acted against. In the end the charges were based on — you will be amazed at this — the "evidence" of a satirical play written by Camille Desmoulins. Desmoulins protested. What he had written was only a play, he said. It was not based on any evidence at all; it was all a **fabrication**, as plays are allowed to be. What happened in his plays, he said, were the extravagances of his imagination — it was only a story. He protested over and over that a play could provide no proof. Despite these protestations, the story formed the basis for the charges against the deputies. Most of the **witnesses** were the original accusers, now all among the leading men of Paris. The trial was held. The judge and jury and the accusers were, evidently, of the same mind. Despite this, the accusations were so very flimsy, and the defenses of the deputies were so very eloquent, that judge, jury, and audience were in no doubt as to their actual innocence.

The judge and jury still intended to convict the deputies. Nothing anyone might have said could have stopped them. Yet they sensed that the audience, despite the fact that they had been hired by the accusers, might protest. These people, despite the money jingling in their pockets, were still human. They were beginning to show signs of compassion. So the judge wrote to the National Convention, saying that both he and the jury feared that there would be trouble if the trial was dragged out any longer. The letter also said that, surely "in a revolutionary process" a long examination of the evidence, for or against, must be unnecessary.

So the Jacobins in the National Convention rose and suggested a decree that said that, in present times, a jury could condemn a person as soon as they felt that they had been "sufficiently instructed" to understand the case and make a judgment. There was some discussion of the validity of such a decree, then the Convention passed the decree. It was, of course, virtually a death **sentence** on anyone who went before a jury.

THE EXECUTION OF THE DEPUTIES

It is hard to believe that the deputies really thought that they would have a fair trial. They had to be executed, because it was the demand for their exclusion from the Convention that set things off and brought the Revolutionary government to power.

The charges, although vague and probably untrue, were not as silly as Helen Williams makes them out to be. The deputies were charged with conspiring with Dumouriez and the Vendéans, and with taking France to war with Europe — which they did, but only in the sense that they were part of the government the countries of Europe declared war upon.

Not surprisingly, the jury in the case of the deputies almost instantly declared itself to be "sufficiently instructed." Sufficiently instructed in what? In the fact that these men were being tried for their value, not their crimes? The condemned men protested at the decision in vain. The court had a decree to support its actions — it felt no need to explain them. Valéze, one of the condemned deputies, was in a rage at the manner of the trial. In a fury, he stabbed himself where he stood in the courtroom. The others were led away to be executed the next day.

The rest of the deputies met their fate with calm and innocence, wishing in their last moments for nothing more than the return of liberty to the Republic. Those who witnessed their last hours, which we did not, for we were in prison, speak much of the impression this calm made on them. It uplifted the spirits of those who were with them to see such brave and dignified behavior. We knew many of these men, and while we did not see them at the last, we can well believe that they behaved to the end with true courage and dignity.

A painting from 1794. It shows some prisoners being brought to face the Revolutionary Tribunal. As the painting shows, the Revolutionary Tribunal became less and less formal and official in the way that it ran things. Originally it should have consisted of a public prosecutor, five judges, and a jury. The men with the spears are soldiers. This leaves about eighteen men for the rest of the officials, and not all of those seem to be paying a lot of attention.

CHAPTER 8

A New Prison

We moved to our new prison just before the execution of the deputies. Our rooms here were entirely bare, so we were allowed to return to our apartment to collect mattresses to sleep on. It was so sad to go back, to see the old rooms, and then to be forced to leave them again. Our new prison was called "Les Anglaises" (the Englishwomen) already, because English **nuns** lived there. As soon as we entered the walls, we were met by a nun who hugged us warmly. This kindness almost reconciled us to the change in accommodation, which was great. Our room was intensely cold and had no stove or chimney. But we were united in this prison by our sex, our circumstances, and our nationality, and we all cared for each other as best we could. At first, the local revolutionary committee was hard on us, for members had been told we were aristocrats. Once we convinced them that we were not, they were less severe with us. They allowed us to walk in the gardens for two hours a day, as long as we were under their supervision.

RELIGION

Attitudes about religion changed between 1779 and 1793.

At first, there was some tolerance of religion, as part of the new liberty. A lot of church property was taken away, but people could worship as they chose. **Convents** and monasteries were left alone; then they were used as prisons.

As time passed, more and more people became **atheists**. Religious groups were treated differently, depending on how many atheists were on the local revolutionary committee.

For a short while, during the Reign of Terror, atheism and Christianity were banned, and worship of the Supreme Being was ordered by Robespierre.

After the fall of Robespierre, the general policy moved back to a limited toleration of religious beliefs.

We talked to them and convinced them that our only crime was being English. They were far kinder than the administrators of police, who also visited regularly. The police forced the nuns to stop wearing their **habits** and **crosses** and to dress as ordinary women. We were allowed visitors. Our French friends brought us news. I was grateful for this, because I had a special reason to fear imprisonment. One of Robespierre's **lackeys**, Barère, had often visited my house in earlier days. He knew I wrote letters home about what was going on. These letters were published in England and translated into French, even read by the Committee of Public Safety. Barère also knew that I knew that he had been in tears on June 3, at the injustice of the action taken against the National Convention. Would he remember? I spent my winter in my new prison with the blade of the guillotine hanging over me, suspended by a single thread.

This picture shows the courtyard of the prison at Bicêtre, in Paris. Helen Williams was lucky in her imprisonment; she did not end up here either. This was a real prison and had been during the reign of Louis XVI. Then it was seen as the worst prison in France, far worse than the Bastille. Those who ran it were said to torture the prisoners, often to the point of killing them.

Its awful reputation got no better with the arrival of the Revolution and liberty. It just had different prisoners. It does not seem that the cruelty of those who ran the prison lessened at all. Most of its prisoners were criminals, beggars, and those whose families had asked for them to be arrested. This suggests that it was partly an asylum for the insane as well. As the picture shows, the prisoners here, male and female, were put in chains.

It was here that the guillotine was tested for the first time, "until it worked properly," which must mean there were several executions when it did not. It was also discovered that all through 1793, the governor here was killing off his prisoners, especially the young boys, by the hundreds.

CHAPTER 9

Madame Roland Is Executed

POLITICAL PARTIES

The extremists who ran the country during the Reign of Terror had gained power in the Montagnard party (see box page 6) by calling themselves Jacobins. Who were the Jacobins, and who opposed them?

Jacobins

The Jacobins began as a club in 1789. Its members wanted a monarchy, led by parliament. More clubs were set up: 5,500 in all. They grew more radical, demanding a republic. Then they were taken over by extremists, like Robespierre. The word "Jacobin" came to mean "extreme."

Girondists

The Girondists (see box page 6) opposed the Jacobins and warned the Convention that both Jacobin and Montagnard groups were too extreme. So the Jacobins hated them. Girondist groups were banned during the Reign of Terror.

It was now that one of the cleverest women in France was executed. I had hoped the day would never come, but it did. Madame Roland was executed. Her husband, a minister to Louis XVI, had gone into hiding, but she had not. She was arrested and thrown into prison. Many people said at the time, meaning to be witty, and yet there was sense in it, that while Monsieur Roland's body was missing, they had managed to capture his soul. She was a very talented lady, very intelligent, and also kind. I can describe her from my own experience, for we were well acquainted. I had gotten to know her when I first arrived in France, and I used to visit her regularly at her **salon**. I have always been very fond of her. She was a great advocate of liberty and very eloquent and graceful in its support. She was tall, shapely, and very dignified. Although she was 35 years old, she was still very handsome to look at. Her dark eyes were very intelligent, and she had a sweet and patient expression.

Her first prison was in Saint Pélagie, and she was shut away before I was also imprisoned, so I was able to visit her, until I myself was shut up. She was still calm and cheerful and talked just as if she were still greeting guests in her salon. She was spending her time reading the few books that she had been allowed to bring with her, and this was what she was doing the first time I arrived to visit her. She told me calmly that she expected to die, that she had no hopes that she would be granted mercy, despite her lifelong support of liberty. She seemed quite prepared to meet her death calmly. Indeed, she was calm all through my visit. Then I asked how her daughter was. Her daughter was only thirteen years old, and she was not with her mother. Here Madame Roland lost her composure. She wept and wept and then said that she did not know where her daughter was; she had had no news of her from friends or even from those who were responsible for her imprisonment.

She was sent to the Conciergerie just before her trial. When she was brought before the Revolutionary Tribunal, she was heroically firm, despite being insulted and badly treated. She dressed all in white, with her dark hair loose and unpowdered and appeared the picture of innocence. Such was her dignified conduct during the course of her trial that she forced from her enemies the tribute of applause and admiration. Before she went to trial, she had sent me papers to smuggle out of the country and publish, to show her innocence, but I had not time to rescue them from their hiding place before my arrest. It does not matter. Her innocence is clear without them. When told of her sentence, she said, "You think me worthy of sharing the fate of the great men you have assassinated. I will try to go to the scaffold with all the courage they have displayed."

On the way to the scaffold, she was composed, even gay, trying to keep up the spirits of her companions. When more than one person was to be executed at the same time, those executed last saw the others die. To be first, was, therefore, a privilege and, as the only woman there, she was told that her name was first on the list. But she said, "Let them go first, to spare them the pain of seeing my blood shed." The executioner said it had been decided that she should go first. "But you cannot, I'm sure, refuse the last request of a lady," she said with a smile. He let her companions go first. When she mounted the scaffold at last, as she was tied to the fatal plank, she lifted up her eyes to the statue of Liberty near the guillotine and cried, "Ah, Liberty! How you've been sported with!"

Roland, who had stayed in hiding until her execution, came out of hiding on hearing of her death and killed himself. Their daughter was safe. She had gone into hiding with friends. She was at liberty when I last heard of her.

A picture of Madame Roland, painted before her imprisonment.

MADAME ROLAND

Madame Roland was a strong supporter of the Revolution and of liberty. Her husband was one of the most important members of the Girondist group (see boxes on pages 6 and 26). Madame Roland had the same beliefs, and she voiced them freely.

But by September 1792, she was already sick of the violent reactions of the more extreme Convention members. She wrote to a friend: "Danton controls everything, and Robespierre is his puppet. If you but knew the awful details of their killing operations! You know of my enthusiasm for the Revolution — well, I am ashamed of it! Its reputation is tarnished by the scoundrels; it is becoming hideous!"

CHAPTER 10

The Reign of Terror Tightens Its Grip

After two months in our new prison, we were released. A young Frenchman, who has since married my sister, managed to get us released by haunting all the officials he could find and finally by begging the release from Chaumette, the **procurer** of the Paris Commune, and a tyrant. So we were free but were watched. We could see very few people and went out little, and yet it was a sort of liberty. We feared to go out, in case, without realizing it, we committed some **transgression** that would lead to being arrested again. We hardly spoke to anyone, for there were spies everywhere, and we jumped at each knock at the door, fearing arrest. For the prisons were growing more crowded daily, and more and more were going to the scaffold as the Reign of Terror tightened its hold. "Suspicion" was now a warrant for imprisonment, and conspiracy and murder were in the air. One man was arrested because he "looked" noble, another because a total stranger swore that he supported monarchy. Some were arrested for having been rich, others for being clever. Many who were arrested asked for the reason in vain. And the numbers of executions rose, and the horrors increased, and the stories of both courage and cowardice were passed from home to home. Yet it seemed to me that there was more courage than cowardice to be found, which gave us hope for humanity even in these dark days.

This picture shows the famous "knitting women." These women were members of the Jacobin clubs when they had become extreme (see box on page 26). This group certainly existed.

They became infamous with the story that they came to the guillotine every day, in large numbers. The story goes that they brought chairs and sat directly in front of the guillotine, knitting away as people were executed. As they knitted, they also jeered at the victims and sometimes spat at them and threw things. Some historians do not believe the story. Most believe that, while some women may have done this, it was not necessarily an everyday ritual for the same group each day. There are historians who say that, considering all the strange things that went on at the time, it is as likely to have happened as not.

Soon after our release from prison, we decided to move from the center of the town to a house in the most remote part of the faubourg, Saint Germain. Our new home was but a few moments walk from the countryside. But although we were close, we did not dare to walk there. The parks and woods that surrounded us and had once belonged to royalty were now haunted by revolutionaries, despots, police spies, even the conspirators themselves on occasion. So we walked in the common fields near our house, where people put their animals to graze. I have no words to describe how reluctantly we returned from our walks to Paris, that den of carnage, that slaughterhouse of man. The guillotine was claiming both the innocent and the guilty alike, and at such a rate that the gutters seemed to stream with blood. And just when it seemed that things could get no worse, when you thought it was not possible to increase the stream of people flowing to the scaffold, you were proved wrong, and the pace of the flow quickened even more.

A few weeks after our release, Rabat Sainte Etienne was executed. He was president of the Committee of Twelve and led the inquiry into the petitions against the 22 deputies that set off the events of May 31 to June 2, 1793. I saw him shortly before he was captured, for he sheltered in our house for a few hours. He was full of despair, not so much for himself as for the country. He and his brother, one of the 73 who signed the petition against the Revolutionary government's decree of June 3, had built themselves a hiding place in the house of a friend, in the wall behind a bookcase, with their own hands. But they had to get a carpenter to fit the door and, though they had confidence in him, the wretch betrayed them, and they were caught. Rabat was brought to the Revolutionary Tribunal and sentenced to death. His brother was sent to the dungeons of the Conciergerie, where he spent many months in a damp cell with only one bed for four of them. Yet he did survive and now sits in the new Convention. The friends who hid them were executed.

At the same time as we heard of Rabat's death, we heard of the death of a young man who died to save his brother. It happened like this. When the names of those who were to go to the scaffold were called out, this young man's brother was not in the room. Thinking of his brother's family, and being himself a single man, he gave himself up to the officer as his brother and was executed in his place. This was despite the fact that his brother was considerably older and looked nothing like him. Such acts were not uncommon in families, and as the number of executions each day was rising, so the check that the officers kept on such things became more slack.

TIMESCALE

The National Convention was taken over by the extremists between May 31 and June 3, 1793. This is when the Reign of Terror began.

Helen Williams was arrested in October 1793. She was released in late November.

Rabat Sainte Etienne was executed on December 5, 1793.

His brother was released in August 1794 and was made a member of the new Convention.

But not everyone died courageously. Madame du Barry, mistress of Louis XV, had fled France at the outbreak of the Revolution but was tricked back to get some hidden jewels. She was arrested and imprisoned by one of the very few Englishmen ever to work for the Revolutionary Tribunal. She knew that prison meant death. But then she was told that if she would only say where she had hidden her treasure, she would be allowed to go free. So she told but was taken to the scaffold anyway. She had to be dragged every inch of the way, and the screaming seemed to go on forever. She was executed at the same time as several bankers, who, despite the fact that they had given all they had to the government as a "patriotic donation," were still executed for having once possessed the money. They went to the scaffold bravely, for now, indeed, to be chosen to die had become a sort of privilege, so far had normality turned itself on its head. Such horrors were taking place that death seemed preferable to life.

Indeed, things had come to such a pass that there was actually an accepted way of dying. Those who, for religious or other reasons, could not face the idea of killing themselves, but yet who wanted to die, followed the same system. They flung open a window or stepped into the street and cried out, "Vive le roi!" [Long live the King!] This was, of course, an instant passport to the scaffold, for if they could not kill themselves, there were many who were willing to lead them to the scaffold and to do the job for them. I must say, at this point, that it was not possible to find out what was going on in the **provinces** or even in the war that was going on. So I cannot say if these horrors were repeated all over France. All I can do is to report events in Paris that I saw or heard of through friends.

The Reign of Terror was taken to the provinces. The most executions were in areas where there was resistance to the Revolution itself, or to the Revolutionary government. The people of towns like Lyons or Nantes, who refused to accept the Revolutionary government, were executed without mercy. The same was true of the Vendée (see pages 10–11). Living in the area was enough to get people's homes and farms destroyed, and often themselves executed as well. The guillotine was not often used. It was too slow. At Nantes, barges full of people were towed out into the river and sunk.

CHAPTER 11

Robespierre

I think I should now pause in my narration of the horrors of the Reign of Terror to give you some picture of the man who was, himself, the main cause of it — Robespierre.

Robespierre was born in Arras, and he and his brothers were left **orphans** at an early age. Yet fortune favored them. They did not suffer such hardships as many orphans do, for they were cared for and educated by the Bishop of Arras, who made sure that they were well looked after. Robespierre won many prizes in his school career, more by diligence and working long hours than by quickness or aptitude. But by the time he was sixteen, he had won enough prizes to have a very good opinion of himself. He and many of those around him expected that he would make his mark on the world by his **eloquence**. He decided to study law, which he felt would be a good profession for him and which would enable him to rise quickly. He and his friends were quickly disappointed, however. He had neither taste nor aptitude for the law, was put off by the least difficulty that was placed in his way, and was not considered to be a good enough public speaker. So the Bishop refused to pay his fees any longer and told him to come back to Arras. After such splendid dreams of success in the capital, this was a great humiliation, which he felt deeply. He brooded on this, secretly, while working as he was told to do.

When he came to power, though, he was able to have his vengeance. He was particularly hard on **men of letters**, perhaps because he was not as eloquent as they were. He even passed a decree against "seditious publications," which came to mean anything that he disliked. So he could stop any play, ban any book, or suppress any performance that he disliked. He asserted that men of letters could not support the revolution, despite protestations that they did, because the very act of writing made them **counterrevolutionary**.

Robespierre did not confine his venom to men of letters but to all those who were excellent in their own sphere. So Lavoisier, the famous chemist, was also condemned for no real reason. He begged that he might have just a little time to finish the experiments he was working on, for, he said, these might be of use to the Revolution.
He was told that the Revolution did not need chemists. Whole families fell to the ax of Robespierre's malice. He had no loyalty to his friends. He seemed to have a ladder of ambition in his head by which he measured people. They had to have enough ambition to do the horrors he commanded without question. But too much of it threatened his position, and then nothing could save them. Desmoulins was an old school friend, Danton had helped Robespierre in his early career, yet they were executed all the same, as soon as they protested about the escalation of the terror.

ROBESPIERRE'S RISE TO POWER

July 20, 1789: made a speech in favor of armed uprisings

1790s: proposed reforms that made him seem in favor of equality, including demands for equal rights for Jews and Blacks

March 31, 1790: was made president of the Jacobins

August 17, 1792: joined the Council of the Paris Commune

May 31–June 2, 1793: took part in overthrow of the Convention

July 27, 1793: joined Committee of Public Safety

December 1793: clearly stated that he favored a policy of terror as a way of governing

May 7, 1794: set up worship of Supreme Being

June 4, 1794: was made president of the Convention. Now Robespierre seemed at the height of his power.

As for his appearance, Robespierre was a little man. He was always neat, even **foppish**, in his way of dressing, despite the fact that he himself insisted that such care in dressing was counterrevolutionary — indeed, there was a time when such a thing as a clean shirt was enough to get this accusation! Yet as I say, he was always neat, with carefully arranged and **powdered hair**, even when the fashion was for disordered, unpowdered hair.

As to a closer description of what he looked like, he had a hideous face. No one who saw him could say otherwise. His eyes, which might be seen to betray the inhuman and foul thoughts that he had, were most often hidden behind a pair of large, green spectacles, despite the fact that he had no need of these, as he had no sight defect. He had a high-pitched voice, and he was quickly moved to angry and passionate speeches.

This portrait of Robespierre, painted before his fall, seems to agree with Helen Williams's statement that he was a neat, careful dresser, with carefully arranged and powdered hair.

Chapter 12

Leaving the City

Now Robespierre began to grow mad with power and suspicious of all those who dared to oppose him. Now no one felt safe. Even his closest friends, those who had worked with him to gain power, were not safe. Indeed, there was reason for some of his fears. For Hébert now came to envy Robespierre and tried to organize a rebellion, the Ventôse, to displace him. He had called the people to rise for Robespierre so many times that he thought that he could raise the people in the same way — ring the bell, beat the drums, call the people to arms, and seize the government. But the plot failed, and he went to the guillotine. Others less guilty followed him. In early April both Danton and Camille Desmoulins were sent to the scaffold after a **farcical** trial. Again the accusation was a lack of support for liberty — when Desmoulins had been the first to wear the red, white, and blue ribbons of the Revolution! Danton had been the one to set up the Revolutionary Tribunal system. But this was nothing when weighed against the fact that both of them had protested against the severity of the Reign of Terror. Several other deputies followed them to the scaffold.

Then it was the turn of the aristocracy and foreigners once again. The Committee of Public Safety decided, on April 15, 1794, that all nobles and foreigners had to leave Paris and other cities within ten days or go to the law. This would have meant the scaffold. We had to decide where to go, then go to our local Revolutionary Tribunal and ask for permission to go there. They would give us a pass allowing us to travel there. This pass would be the mark of Cain to us; wherever we went, it would ensure us bad treatment. We chose a village not far from Paris and said good-bye to our sister, who, having married her Frenchman, did not have to leave the city. Once more we left our homes and said good-bye to our neighbors, who wept to see us go. We had to pass through the Square of the Revolution to leave the city, where we had a good view of the scaffold, the crowds, and the same dreary daily procession of human misery going to lose their lives. We reached the barrier, only to find ourselves in a huge mass of carriages, all trying to leave in time. Most people had left their departure until the last minute, so the demand for carriages was great, the supply both small and expensive. Some were reduced to traveling by cart with their furniture or using all manner of rickety vehicles. We did not reach our new home until sunset. We could still just see Paris in the distance. We feared that this decree was just the first step in a general arrest and execution of nobles and foreigners, and so it was. We were arrested, but the revolutionary committee of our village were kind to us. They managed to arrange for us to have passes to return to Paris and live there. This meant that when decrees were passed for the execution of nobles and foreigners outside of Paris, they did not apply to us. We owe them our lives, yet it was not a happy return.

TIMETABLE

Hébert and his followers don't seem to have been as rebellious as Helen Williams says. But they were certainly accused of plotting an uprising. There was growing discontent with the government.

March 13, 1794: Hébert and his followers were arrested.
March 24, 1794: Hébert and his followers were executed.
March 31, 1794: deputies Danton, Desmoulins, La Croix, and Philippeaux were arrested.
April 5, 1794: deputies were executed.
April 16, 1794: law against foreigners and nobles living in Paris, towns on the coast, or towns with city walls

Paris was now a never-ending stream of executions; the smell of blood hung in the air. People were being brought to trial "on suspicion of being suspected." No one could feel safe now. A deep and silent gloom pervaded the once happy city. Most people watched the processions of death with a stupefied horror. What could they do? They could not stop the executions. They could not even show horror or sympathy, for they saw no one was safe. Not even in their own homes, with their own families, could they dare to speak out, in case they were overheard. If they did anything even remotely out of step, it would be their feet on the steps to the scaffold, their neck beneath the blade of the guillotine. Life was so difficult and dangerous that many killed themselves or got themselves executed. Crying "Vive le roi!" was now joined by a new cry: "Down with the tyrant!"

But amidst all the horror there was the occasional act of humanity, the occasional **reprieve**. Sometimes these came too late, sometimes just in time. One young man was granted a pardon, and the officer who had to deliver it hurried to the prison where he was held, only to be told that his cart had already left for the scaffold. He ran after it, crying out, "Reprieve!" But it reached the scaffold. He ran on, calling all the while through the crowd. The blade fell. He ran on, now with no breath to cry out. The blade rose and fell again. And again it rose and fell, as he pushed through the crowd. There was but one left, and the messenger hauled himself up the steps and asked the young man his name. It was not the right one. The others executed had been women. Leaving the young man to his fate, he went back to the prison, where the cart was loading up again. Here he found and released the right young man to the wife and nine children who had come to bid him farewell.

A painting of an execution, done at the time. The statue on the right is of Liberty. People are cheering as the victim, tied to a board, with his hair cut short and his hands tied behind him, is laid under the blade. As the pace of the executions increased, the prisoners were not only brought to the scaffold by the cartload, they were sometimes also made to line up, up the steps, to speed up the process.

Changing the Days

Among the extraordinary changes that had taken place in France by this time were changes both to the calendar and to religion. The change in the calendar was so pleasing and mild compared to all the other innovations, such as the guillotine, that it quite captured the imagination. Nivôse is now the month of snows. Floréal is the month of flowers. This calendar was introduced in my days of captivity, and I soon learned how to use it, although as the new months did not quite overlap with the old, it was somewhat confusing at first. It was, however, vital that I learn it, for all communications with the authorities had to be dated in the new calendar correctly before they would even be read, let alone thought about. The days of the week changed as well, and the way the years ran. They were all "rationalized." So now there were ten days in a week, and the last of these, decadi, was a sort of Sunday, for this was the only day when the guillotine did not work. On these days, those who worked the guillotine were often to be seen on the former royal parks, like those I mentioned near where we moved to, enjoying themselves or taking part in the **pagan** celebrations that, soon after the replacement of the calendar, came to replace the old religion.

So we were now to worship a deity called the Supreme Being, and the first festival in the name of this new god was to be a grand affair. It was designed by David, the painter lackey of Robespierre. Paris was decked out in wreaths of branches and flowers, all woven with ribbons bearing the colors of France. The Convention marched in procession with bands, and all wore tricolored plumes in their hats and carried bunches of fruit and flowers. A great amphitheater was put up in the garden of the Tuilleries in front of the palace, and Robespierre made a speech about universal nature, virtue, and the possibility of immortality — within sight of the scaffold!

A painting of the Festival of the Supreme Being, the later part, held in the Champ de Mars. The festival was held on June 8, 1794. Notice the statue of Wisdom and Philosophy, and the man-made mound that Robespierre spoke from. The palace where the first part of the ceremony was held is the big building on the left in the background.

When the foul fiend had finished his mocking speech, he walked up to a strange shape put up in front of the palace, a monstrous figure with ass's ears. We had been wondering what it was for. He now announced it was atheism, which he said was as bad as the old religion. He set it alight, and in its place was put a beautifully formed statue to represent wisdom and philosophy. We now all marched to the Champ de Mars, where, with much cost and effort, a rocky summit had been made. From there he made another speech, and the festival closed with hymns and songs to the Supreme Being.

So now people were married at the altar of Hymen, and Notre Dame Cathedral became a Temple of Reason, with priestesses who served the goddess of Reason and the goddess of Liberty. These were represented by actresses from a nearby theater. Besides adopting the new religion, people were encouraged to mock the old, with mock processions, and the burning of all saintly **relics**, scraps of cloth, bones, even a spoon and plate believed to have belonged to Jesus. Arms, legs, toes, and fingers of martyrs, and all these relics were thrown into bonfires, and many people watched them burn with satisfaction.

Yet the new religion only lasted a short time, and many who had eagerly accepted it, all in the spirit of **conformity**, were then executed for "suspected beliefs."

THE NEW CALENDAR	
The months of the year did not exactly match. The months began between the 19th and the 22nd of one month and covered most of the next. They are usually referred to by the names of the months they covered most of.

January	Pluvôse
February	Ventôse
March	Germinal
April	Floréal
May	Prairial
June	Messidor
July	Thermidor
August	Fructidor
September	Vendemiaire
October	Brumaire
November	Frimaire
December	Nivôse

The week was made up of ten days, which were referred to by number. Decadi, the last day of the ten, was treated as a day of rest.

CHAPTER 13

Drunk with Blood

We have now reached the point when the tyrant, grown bolder by success, drunk with power, and with no regard for legality, reaches the climax of his crimes and accelerates his fall. Two days after the Festival of the Supreme Being, Robespierre passed a law allowing the Revolutionary Tribunal to condemn any brought to them as they pleased, with no defense and no trial. From now until the fall of Robespierre, the "trials" of the Revolutionary Tribunal were no more than a formal reading of the list of names of those to be executed. Those brought to trial were not allowed to speak. When they tried to speak, they were mostly ignored. The occasional reply was often worse than silence. For instance, when one woman, accused of a plot against the Revolutionary government, protested that she had never been to the place where she and the plotters were supposed to have met, she got an answer. It was, "Well, if you had been there you would certainly have been part of the conspiracy, so you may as well die with the rest." And that was the end of her trial. She went to the scaffold with the others.

From now on, the prisons were places of horror and despair. They were stuffed with more and more people, to bursting point. People no longer went to the guillotine in ones, twos, sixes at the most. Now people were called to fill several carts a day, which transported them to the guillotine, ten at a time. One day, 159 people were taken from the Luxembourg, where I had been in prison, to the Conciergerie to be executed the next day. This was upon the pretense of a plot laid in the prison, though there was no evidence of any such thing. What danger could these poor prisoners have been, anyway?

PRISON PLOTS
Helen Williams was lucky to have been moved from the Luxembourg prison. One of the prison plots that she talks about was supposed to have been hatched in the Luxembourg in April 1794. The "plotters" were probably the 159 people that she says were taken to the Conciergerie in one batch.

Very few of the "plots" that were said to have been hatched would have been any real danger to the Revolutionary government. It would be more surprising, in the circumstances, if prisoners did not discuss ways of overthrowing the government!

The events of the Reign of Terror seemed to confirm what many people who supported the monarchy, and the other countries of Europe, had said all along — the ideas of liberty and equality could not work. Because of the cruelties of the aristocracy and the deprivations of the poor before the Revolution, there were, from the beginning, a good many people who wanted only revenge. They wanted the good things they had never had, and now they could take them. This was something that some people had stressed about the Revolution from the very beginning. This picture shows the looting of the king's wine cellars in 1782. It was painted by Zoffany, a supporter of the monarchy, in about 1783. It is suggesting that if you give the poor liberty, they will use it to kill, steal, and do everything to excess.

CHAPTER 15

Escape!

ÉMIGRÉS

Émigrés were French people who left to live in another country. Some of them joined the armies of other countries to fight the new government. Others just waited for a chance to return home.

There were two waves of émigrés. The first was mostly royalist nobles who left in 1789, after the Bastille was stormed.

The second wave was in 1792. It started after the September massacres. These massacres happened after rumors spread that the Austrians were marching on Paris. About 1,000 prisoners in various prisons were executed — they were said to support the Austrians. This time many of the émigrés were people who had supported the Revolution but who were not happy with the bloodthirsty turn events were taking.

As I have said, I was worried all through this period, for I knew that the articles I had written about the Revolution had been published in the English papers, and that my name had been happily subscribed to them. These papers were translated into French, so that the Committee of Public Safety could read what the English were saying about them. What if they should connect my name with this other Helen Williams, as surely someone must do, some day?

I had twice endured imprisonment, each time wondering if my name on a list might prompt someone's memory. And our exile from Paris would have ended in our execution, had not the humane members of the revolutionary committee not offered us a way to return to Paris, with official passes to allow us to remain. Yet there was no knowing if we would once again be arrested on the whim of someone or another, for the causes of arrest were so slight. And, as so many made their way to the guillotine, totally innocent of any crime against the Revolutionary government, it seemed all but impossible that I should remain free and unharmed.

Even worse than the fears that I had about the possibility of my arrest were the fears that began to haunt me about the danger I might pose to my own family. I felt sure that my sister especially, having married a Frenchman, was bound to be safer if no one connected her with me. I began to fear that my presence in the city made it more likely that all the rest of my family would come to harm, that they would be seen as conspirators, not innocent women, if I was discovered to be living among them.

Then I was offered the chance to escape. It would mean leaving my family, for the offer was made to me alone. Yet they were not in the danger I was in and said they would be happier if I was gone. So I left Paris once again, haunted by images of pursuit, feeling that it was impossible that I would actually escape. I felt as if there was a magic spell that would chain my feet at the **frontier** of France, an impassable boundary. As the frontier got nearer, I became more agitated. At Bourg Libre, the last French post where they had commissaries to examine passports and those who presented them, my heart sank within me. I tried to resign myself to the inevitable, to the return to Paris, and all that would follow.

But I found that I had worried in vain. The Revolutionary government found itself most stretched at the frontiers. The frontier officers barely glanced at our papers before letting us through. Basle was the next stop. Some tall stakes were driven into the ground to mark the exact boundary of France and Switzerland. We drove past them and were, at last, beyond the reach of the Revolutionary government, beyond the reach of the guillotine.

In Basle, I was
safe yet far from
either friends or
family. And here I stayed
until, far sooner than I would
have thought possible, I had news of the fall
of Robespierre, a fall that was to bring peace and consolation to
so many of my fellow creatures. Yet when I had left, he had seemed
secure at the height of his power. I had sworn never to return to
France until he was destroyed, and this seemed as if it would be
never. Yet now, a few weeks later, as it seemed, he was toppled, and I
was free to return to Paris. I was grateful but also full of wonder.
How had this come about? After waiting to be sure that the struggle
between the rest of Robespierre's Jacobins and the National
Convention was well decided, and decided in favor of the
Convention, I decided to return to Paris.

*One of the most
surprising things
about Helen Williams's
account is that she waited so
long before trying to escape. From
the outbreak of the Revolution there
had been many people, French and
foreign, who had tried to escape
from France. Many aristocrats, who
had their castles looted at the start
of the Revolution, escaped as best
they could and made their way to
other countries to wait for a better
time to go home. Many went to
England. At first, they were allowed,
even encouraged, to leave. But as
the Reign of Terror took hold,
escape became more difficult.*

CHAPTER 16

How Robespierre Fell

On entering again the polluted city, it was difficult not to remember a thousand horrid scenes. As I drove along the Rue Sainte Honore, the appalling procession to the guillotine arose again; I saw in the vehicles of death the ghosts of my murdered friends. The magnificent Square of the Revolution appeared to be clotted with blood and full of the dead. Along the silent, deserted streets of the faubourg, Saint Germain, I saw over the gates of every lodging house and hôtel the words "proprieté national" [property of the nation]. Red flags still fluttered everywhere. They reminded me of a novel by Daniel Defoe, where he describes the red crosses that were painted on the doors of houses in England during the plague of 1665. Yet now, at least, there was hope of recovery. While there were still acts of revenge and retribution, humanity and mercy were now at work.

As to the tyrant's fall, it came about through his own excesses. Following his decree that allowed for execution without trial, the Revolutionary Tribunal and the guillotine sped up their pace still more. And as people were hurried from the prisons to the guillotine, there were many mistakes made in identity, many people either called in the place of others or taken because a name on a list had been misread. If, for some reason, the officer calling the names had a dislike for a particular prisoner, then his name would be called, whether it was on the list or not.

The system became very **lax**. "After all," the jailers might have said, "what does it matter? They are all going to die anyway, if they are in prison." And this feeling infected the victims themselves. Few of the prisoners protested at the mistakes when they were made. They, too, felt that it did not matter. There was no avoiding execution, and most of them were in on false charges anyway. They had no illusions that protests might bring them justice; they had learned otherwise long before.

While all this was going on, in early Prairial, a plot to kill Robespierre failed. A few days later, a girl, Amée Cecile Renaud, who was just nineteen years old, had the courage that an armed nation lacked. She entered the room of the tyrant alone and unarmed to try to show him the oppression the country groaned under. She was arrested, and all the other members of her family were arrested, too. They were all taken to the Conciergerie and questioned. They were accused of plotting to kill Robespierre, even though the girl was unarmed. So they were "tried," convicted in an instant, and sent to their death at the guillotine. They were not allowed to speak, but they were wrapped in the red cloaks that were kept for those who had committed especially severe crimes and bundled off with haste, along with 69 other people, to their deaths.

TIMETABLE, 1794

May 24: attempt by Amée Cecile Renaud to kill Robespierre. Despite what Helen Williams says, Renaud was armed with two knives.
June 4: Robespierre was made president of the Convention.
June 10: decree that allowed for execution without trial
June 28: Robespierre called "a tyrant" in the Convention
July 3: Robespierre left a debate in a huff because he was argued with and did not go to the Convention for several days.
July 27: the Convention ordered the arrest of Robespierre and his friends. They were taken to the Luxembourg. The jailer refused to lock them up. They left and went to the Town Hall to plan their next move. They could have beaten the Convention, but the Paris Commune did not help in time. They were declared to be outlaws and arrested again.

Luckily for France, though, the tyrant did fall, and it was even more satisfying to know that he met his end at the guillotine, his own evil instrument, rather than simply at the hands of an assassin. He thought himself totally above the law, able to do exactly as he pleased. So he made a move to execute yet more members of the Convention and found himself arrested in his turn. And, as he himself had made sure, there was only one consequence of arrest — death.

So now Paris rebuilds itself, and we try to forget. Liberty is now slowly reasserting her true nature. But I have seen such sights as cannot be forgotten. I have seen the cells of the Conciergerie, looked at its walls, some stained with blood, seen the room where the condemned had had their hair cut off, their hands tied, and their necks bared for the blade. It is a horror that will never leave me.

AFTER THE ARREST
July 28 (early morning): The Convention made Robespierre and his friends outlaws and arrested them at the Town Hall. Now either Robespierre was shot, or he shot himself. He was wounded.
July 28: Robespierre and 21 friends went to the guillotine.
July 29: 70 more were executed.

A painting showing the arrest of Robespierre and his friends at the Town Hall. It was dark, and things were very confused. It is easy to see why it is not clear whether he was shot, or he shot himself.

The Rights of Man

We, the representatives of the people in the National Assembly, consider that a disregard for the rights of man is the sole cause of bad government. So we have set out the natural rights of man as we see them, to remind all those who govern how they should behave to promote the happiness and security of all.

1. Men are born and remain free and equal in rights. Social distinctions between them should only be made for the good working of society.

2. Those who make political groups should do so to preserve the rights of man, rights to liberty, property, security, and to resist oppression.

3. No man or group of men can exercise power that has not been given to them by the people.

4. Liberty of action should not be allowed to harm others. One man should not be able to harm another while exercising his rights. So these rights should be set by the law, to be fair.

5. The law can only forbid actions that are harmful to society. No one can be forced to do anything the law does not demand or be made to stop doing what it does not forbid.

6. All citizens have a right to take part in lawmaking. This may be personally or through representatives they choose. The law applies equally to everyone.

7. A person can only be arrested for breaking the law, and arrest, imprisonment, trial, and punishment should be conducted as the law demands. No one should issue his own instructions or act outside of the law.

8. The law must only punish where strictly necessary.

9. Every man is presumed innocent until he is found guilty. No undue force should be used in his arrest, imprisonment, or at any other time.

10. People may have what political and religious beliefs they choose, as long as they are within the law.

11. People are allowed to publish or speak publicly about their beliefs, as long as they do not break the law to do so.

12. To guarantee the rights of man, there has to be a police force; this force must work for the good of everyone, not to its own advantage.

13. Money will be needed to run the country; this will be raised in taxes from the people, according to what they are able to pay.

14. All people, either in person or through their representatives, can demand to be shown why such taxes are necessary and how they are spent.

15. Everyone who takes part in the running of the country is responsible to the people for his actions and can be questioned about them at any time.

16. If a society does not have a guarantee of the rights of its people, and if it has power in the hands of one person, then it does not have a constitution.

17. People have a right to their own property; they cannot be deprived of it unless the law demands this, and even so, they have to be compensated for the loss.

THE RIGHTS OF MAN
The text of the Rights of Man has been simplified from the original, but all of the rights are here. It is hard to see how they could have become so misused as to produce the Reign of Terror.

In fact, the only way that it works is if the laws are fair, for it is the laws that lay out what people's rights are. So if people can change the laws, then they can claim that they are still behaving properly, because they are acting as the laws tell them to.

DÉCLARATION
DES DROITS DE L'HOMME
ET DU CITOYEN,

Décretés par l'Assemblée Nationale dans les séances des 20.21.
23.24 et 26 août 1789, acceptés par le Roi

PRÉAMBULE

LES représentans du peuple Francois, constitués en assemblée nationale, considérant que l'ignorance, l'oubli ou le mépris des droits de l'homme sont les seules causes des malheurs publics et de la corruption des gouvernemens ont résolu d'exposer dans une déclaration solemnelle, les droits naturels, inaliénables et sacrés de l'homme, afin que cette déclaration, constamment présente à tous les membres du corps social, leur rappelle sans cesse leurs droits et leurs devoirs; afin que les actes du pouvoir legislatif et ceux du pouvoir exécutif, pouvant être à chaque instant comparés avec le but de toute institution politique, en soient plus respectés; afin que les reclamations des citoyens, fondées désormais sur des principes simples et incontestables, tournent toujours au maintien de la constitution et du bonheur de tous.

EN conséquence, l'assemblée nationale reconnoît et déclare, en présence et sous les auspices de l'Etre suprême les droits suivans de l'homme et du citoyen.

ARTICLE PREMIER.

LES hommes naissent et demeurent libres et égaux en droits, les distinctions sociales ne peuvent être fondées que sur l'utilité commune.

II.

LE but de toute association politique est la conservation des droits naturels et imprescriptibles de l'homme; ces droits sont la liberté, la propriété, la sureté, et la résistance à l'oppression.

III.

LE principe de toute souveraineté réside essentiellement dans la nation, nul corps, nul individu ne peut exercer d'autorité qui n'en émane expressement.

IV.

LA liberté consiste à pouvoir faire tout ce qui ne nuit pas à autrui. Ainsi, l'exercice des droits naturels de chaque homme, n'a de bornes que celles qui assurent aux autres membres de la société la jouissance de ces mêmes droits; ces bornes ne peuvent être déterminées que par la loi.

V.

LA loi n'a le droit de défendre que les actions nuisibles à la société. Tout ce qui n'est pas défendu par la loi ne peut être empêché, et nul ne peut être contraint à faire ce qu'elle n'ordonne pas.

VI.

LA loi est l'expression de la volonté générale; tous les citoyens ont droit de concourir personnellement, ou par leurs représentans, à sa formation; elle doit être la même pour tous, soit qu'elle protege, soit qu'elle punisse. Tous les citoyens étant égaux à ses yeux, sont également admissibles à toutes dignités, places et emplois publics, selon leur capacité, et sans autres distinction que celles de leurs vertus et de leurs talens.

VII.

NUL homme ne peut être accusé, arreté, ni détenu que dans les cas déterminés par la loi, et selon les formes qu'elle a prescrites. ceux qui sollicitent, expédient, exécutent ou font exécuter des ordres arbitraires, doivent être punis; mais tout citoyen appelé ou saisi en vertu de la loi, doit obéir à l'instant, il se rend coupable par la résistance.

VIII.

LA loi ne doit établir que des peines strictement et évidemment nécessaires, et nul ne peut être puni qu'en vertu d'une loi établie, et promulguée antérieurement au délit, et légalement appliquée.

IX.

TOUT homme étant présumé innocent jusqu'à ce qu'il ait été déclaré coupable, s'il est jugé indispensable de l'arrêter, toute rigueur qui ne serait pas nécessaire pour s'assurer de sa personne doit être sévèrement réprimée par la loi.

X.

NUL ne doit être inquiété pour ses opinions, mêmes religieuses pourvu que leur manifestation ne trouble pas l'ordre public établi par la loi.

XI.

LA libre communication des pensées et des opinions est un des droits les plus precieux de l'homme; tout citoyen peut donc parler écrire, imprimer librement; sauf à répondre de l'abus de cette liberté dans les cas déterminés par la loi.

XII.

LA garantie des droits de l'homme et du citoyen nécessite une force publique; cette force est donc instituée pour l'avantage de tous, et non pour l'utilité particuliere de ceux à qui elle est confiée.

XIII.

POUR l'entretien de la force publique, et pour les dépenses d'administration, une contribution commune est indispensable; elle doit être également répartie entre les citoyens en raison de leurs facultées.

XIV.

LES citoyens ont le droit de constater par eux même ou par leurs représentans, la nécessité de la contribution publique, de la consentir librement, d'en suivre l'emploi, et d'en déterminer la quotité, l'assiette, le recouvrement et la durée.

XV.

LA société a le droit de demander compte à tout agent public de son administration.

XVI.

TOUTE société, dans laquelle la garantie des droits n'est pas assurée, ni les séparation des pouvoirs déterminée, n'a point de constitution

XVII.

LES propriétés étant un droit inviolable et sacré, nul ne peut en être privé, si ce n'est lorsque la nécessité publique, légalement constatée, l'exige évidemment, et sous la condition d'une juste et préalable indemnité.

AUX REPRESENTANS DU PEUPLE FRANCOIS

Glossary

All definitions refer to the use of the word in the 1790s.

assassination   to kill someone, usually a famous person, violently. Usually done by one person, acting alone, for money, political, or religious reasons.

atheism   not believing in a god or a life after death of any kind.

charge   an accusation made by the court.

civil war   fighting between groups of people in one country that involves the whole country.

Committee of Public Safety   set up on April 6, 1793, this committee began with nine members and was supposed to suggest to the Convention how the country should be run. During the Reign of Terror, it had twelve members and ran the country. The Convention did not dare to argue with it.

conformity   doing the same as most other people.

constitution   the basic principles and laws of a nation and the guaranteed rights of its citizens.

convent   a place where nuns live.

counterrevolutionary   at first this meant "against the ideas of the Revolution," but during the Reign of Terror, it came to be applied to any act that the Revolutionary government disapproved of. It was used as an excuse to arrest a person, so almost any act could be called "counterrevolutionary."

crosses   these symbols were worn on chains around the necks of the nuns.

decree   an order by a government that has to be obeyed as if it were law.

départements   areas of France that are similar to counties in the United States.

denounce   to accuse someone publicly of a crime.

deputies   the representatives of the people — those who were elected to the National Convention.

eloquence   being able to speak and express ideas well.

fabrication   something that is made up.

faction   a group of people, inside of a larger group, who all have the same goals. The things that they want are often not the same things that the larger group wants.

farcical   silly and pointless.

faubourg   an area around Paris, either just outside or just inside the city walls, but not in the center of the city.

foppish   too concerned about appearance, too fashionable, clean, etc.

frontier   the border between one country and another.

Girondists   the reformers who wanted reform without bloodshed. They had the most influence on the Convention that was broken up over May 31 to June 2, 1793. They came back to power when the Reign of Terror ended.

habit   a nun's uniform.

improbable   unlikely.

individual liberties   the freedom of each person to believe what they like and to say what they believe.

inquiry   when a group of people investigate something that needs explaining or sorting out.

Jacobins   the name given to groups of people that believed different things at different times during the French Revolution. The Jacobins first wanted a monarch who would work with parliament to run the country. Then they wanted a republic. Then they were slowly taken over by those people who wanted to rule by terror.

lackeys   actually meant a type of servant but is used here to mean people who would follow a particular person, agreeing with them and doing whatever they say.

lax   not efficient; making many mistakes.

local administration   in the Reign of Terror, the local administration was made up of the revolutionary committees.

maligned   people who are maligned are lied about and falsely accused by people who want to harm them.

men of letters   well-educated people.

minister   a person who helps a king or queen rule.

monarchy   a country ruled by a king or queen.

Montagnards   the party that took over the Convention between May 31 and June 2, 1793. The Montagnards believed that it was necessary to rule by terror until the French Revolution had succeeded, and until it could not be beaten. It was while they ran the Convention that the Reign of Terror took place.

National Assembly   the French Parliament before the Revolution. It had representatives of the nobles, the churchmen, and the people. The representatives of the people had very little influence on the laws it made.

National Convention   the French Parliament after the Revolution. It was made up just of representatives of the people, sent in from all areas of France.

nuns   devout women who live together in a convent and worship God.

orphan   a child, one or both of whose parents are dead.

pagan   a word used by Christians to describe people or things that are not Christian.

Paris Commune   the town council of Paris during the Revolution that took over on July 14, 1789, having thrown out the old council.

petition   an official letter to the people running the country, asking for something. Petitions are signed by everyone who agrees with the request.

powdered hair   the fashion at the time (for men or women), was to arrange your hair in the way that you wanted it, (or even wear a wig) and then to dust it all over with a fine white or gray powder, until the original hair color was hidden.

procurer   one of the most important members of the Paris Commune.

provinces   used to refer to the rest of France outside Paris, especially the countryside.

rebellion   an armed uprising against whoever is governing the country.

relics   something that is supposed to be part of a holy person's body, or something they owned that is worshiped after they are dead.

reprieve   a delay, or even a cancellation of a sentence of execution.

republic   a country that is ruled by a group elected by the people of the country.

Revolutionary Tribunal   the court in Paris, set up on March 10, 1793, to speed up the trials of counterrevolutionaries.

revolutionary army   not a real army, but the people sent out into France on March 10, 1793, to make sure that the revolutionary committees in the départements were being strict enough.

revolutionary committees   set up in each area of Paris and all through France to run local life.

royalists   people who believe the country should be run by a king or queen.

salon   a large room in a grand house. Some ladies in France at the time used to have meetings at their houses that were a cross between meetings and a party. These meetings were referred to as salons, after the room where they often took place.

sentence   the decision of the court as to how a person should be punished.

transgression   breaking the law.

treason   an act against whoever is governing the country.

Vendée   an area in the west of France where an uprising began with the intent of bringing back the monarchy.

witnesses   people who are called in to court to give evidence, usually about something they are supposed to have seen.

Index

Numbers in *italic* type refer to captions and pictures; numbers in **bold** type refer to information boxes.